# Contents

Queen Mother (Cover)

*Made for her 90th birthday for the Henley Festival. This lady has been as benign a presence to the exhibition as the real Queen Mother has been to the country.*

Collages (Inside cover pages)

*The pages at the front and end of this book are all, without exception, the work of people young and old on their first encounter with the method of modelling with wire and paper. It shows as nothing else could, that this is a method that is open to everyone, and not, I repeat, not for the specialist only. This may well mean yourself.*

Published by The Surrey Institute of Art & Design, University College. Copyright © 1999 Peter Rush

ISBN: 1-899817-01-8

# Foreword

The launch of 'Rush on Paper' offers a timely reminder of the ability of art to confront us with deeper truths without words. Published by The Surrey Institute of Art & Design, University College, in collaboration with the artist, 'Rush on Paper' is a book to be enjoyed at many levels. It presents an overview of Peter Rush's paper sculpture, while, eminently practical, offering an in depth insight into the unique paper technique, which is the hallmark of his work.

Developed by the artist, this paper technique allows literally anyone to become excited about the medium, stimulated by the method and equipped to create sculpture with unusual effects. During Peter's countless popular workshops, the step-by-step process, illustrated in the book, has been experienced with great delight by many hundreds of people of all ages and abilities. No further recommendations are needed: this is art for all.

At the same time, 'Rush on Paper', covers the enormous breadth of the artist's work with beautiful photography. The book was launched in the Foyer Gallery with a touring exhibition of new work to celebrate the millennium, titled: 'Rush on Them – Parodies in Paper'. As always, Peter's applied magic manages to pinpoint the mesmerising power of the bully, while zooming in on their fragile egos, a combination that makes for political and material success. In us the viewers, fear, awe and pity struggle for supremacy. Do they terrify us into submission or do we take the easy option out and allow spin to deceive us?

Including life-size, smaller cased, and interactive sculptures, the work brought together in 'Rush on Them' marks a departure from gentle humour into the more acerbic arena of parody and satire. Many public figures which have been given the Rush treatment will be instantly recognisable. Yet, disguised by jolly appearances something sinister has crept into the plot: all is not what it seems with 'Them'.

**Christine Kapteijn**
Galleries Co-ordinator
Foyer Gallery / James Hockey Gallery
The Surrey Institute of Art & Design, University College

# An introduction to modelling wire & paper figures

Twenty years ago I wrote a book on modelling with paper. It described an approach that I had put together myself and since then I have discovered a great deal more.

This use of softened paper as a modelling material, directly applied on to a chicken wire frame-work came about as the result of a desperate bid on my part to lead a more interesting life. More interesting than the passive and sedentary life of the twenty previous years as an illustrator of children's books and children's television. Lovely work but it had necessitated long hours chained to a drawing table, only Radio Four and the studio cat accompanying those long solitary working sagas going far into the night.

This imposed isolation was not healthy for a nature already taciturn and I began casting around for a way of escape. Lacking courage to generally announce my retirement, I began, instead, to become awkward. No longer easy going, I began quarrelling with those who had kindly supplied me with work all those years, petulantly demanding terms and conditions I knew to be unreasonable. At first they would try to accommodate me, for old times' sake, but soon looked elsewhere. My self-torpedoed career as a television and book illustrator listed horribly and sank. Had it not, I never would have freed myself and I have, not once, regretted it.

As a relief from unending drawing I had always played about with modelling paper, using the method I had evolved myself some years earlier and it was this I turned to now. Initially I made small detailed models to photograph for book and magazine covers. Later they were used to illustrate news items on television and I found myself heading straight back to the life I thought I had left behind.

In the end I just made paper and wire models entirely for my own interest; these were usually people, usually life-size. I earned money for a growing family by working as a caricaturist, using the figures to draw attention to myself. This caricaturing kept the drawing going, making it more spontaneous, and kept the 'observing eye' employed.

At the end of ten years I had so many unsold and seemingly unsaleable figures hanging around the house and studio, that they had naturally formed themselves into an exhibition and, thanks to the perspicacity of Caroline Mornement (who has also helped with this book), this exhibition has travelled up and down the country, hired by Art Centres, City Museums and Galleries almost continuously these last four years. Workshops for all ages are usually run in conjunction with the exhibitions (these are quite often in schools where there can be up to a hundred children or more at a time).

I have become increasingly aware of the privilege that goes with introducing all manner of people to this modelling technique. My respect for a medium that enables so many people to bring their models through with such success is continually reconfirmed. Such results are a tribute to the marvellous sensitivity of this softened-moulded humble kitchen roll and the startling graphic qualities of papers like typing and copy paper. They trigger off dormant, but quite unsullied, tactile memory in us, and it is this awakened intelligence that lends such authority to our work.

This unstinting good nature of paper enables me cheerfully to devote my working life (and much of the rest of it also) to introducing others, talented or otherwise, to the straight-forward method, I have tried to describe in the following pages.

**Peter Rush**

(1-2) The Tory Party

*A Tricerotops was made for the Labour Party to ride on but, having lost that particular election, I also lost interest in modelling them.*

1

2

(3-5) The New Labour Party
Tony Blair (3), John Prescott (4) & Robin Cook (5) (details)

*John Prescott and Tony Blair hang on springs from a bar.*
*The up-and-down motion causes movements of head and arms*
*from fixed wires. The figures spin and whirl, and Robin Cook*
*furiously flaps his wings.*

## Tools

*Long-nosed pliers*, *tin snips* or *heavy duty scissors* (old) used for cutting chicken wire.

*Garden gloves* are handy for this also.

*Drill* (hand or electric) and fine drill bit.

*Glue gun* – marvellous for binding different kinds of materials together. It also has a repertoire of useful effects, but if it dribbles on you it can give you quite a severe burn.

*Hot air gun* (paint-stripper) or *hair drier* for fast, superficial drying.

*Spray diffuser* – for spraying inks or thin colour for delicate effects; this also gets paint where a brush cannot. Inexpensive from art shops.

## Materials

*Chicken wire fine gauge* 1/2" from Garden Centres or DIY shops.

*Solid wooden block* (rough) for base.

*Length of fencing wire,* about as thick as a match stick. Some fine *garden wire.*

*White emulsion* – reasonable quality.

*Wallpaper paste* – cellulose.

*Kitchen roll* – medium quality white, unpatterned.

Sheets of *typing paper, copy paper, exercise book paper.*

Tubes of gold, bronze, silver, *acrylic, gouache, poster paints.*

*Coloured inks* are useful.

*Gold powder* if you can find some – (try good art shops & theatre suppliers).

*Soft brushes* – several – nylon.

*Good visual reference.*

*Working area* – small table with good, fresh, all-round light (not fluorescent) – work is best done at eye-level, so you may need a heavy box or similar on the table.

## Decision time – what to make?

If you are undecided, start with something you are already familiar with:

*A pet or animal perhaps.*
*Or person with whose image you are saturated.*
*A portrait head with hands.*
*A famous face.*
*Caricature.*
*Figure in action in an appropriate setting.*
*Two figures interacting.*
*A vivid incident that has stayed in the mind and needs exorcising.*
*An insect, bird, cockerel, lizard, lobster.*
*People metamorphosing.*
*Fantasy figures.*

Almost anything that can be 'visualised' is 'achievable' (given time and attention). With this in mind I would encourage you to do something dynamic that has nicely observed detail. We can change this model of ours at any time, quite radically, and are not obliged to stay with the first idea.

Still unsure?

Start with a costumed figure 12" (30cms) high.

# A figure in action: the basic technique

The following methods have evolved over twenty years or so and have proved themselves to be reliable. However, nothing is static, and it may be that you see a way of doing something, or another material, that is more effective than those described. Also, some of you trying this work may be very young, so I apologise for sounding patronising, although often it is the children who pick it up straight away, and others, who have a history in different media, like clay and plaster, have to work hard to appreciate how different modelling paper is. However, no matter what the approach, you will find that the 'self-teaching' element is very apparent, I am happy to tell you.

## Wooden Base and Armature

Drill a hole about $1/2$" deep in your block of wood, off-centre and toward one end. Cut a length of the stiff wire 14" long and straighten it. Force it into the hole. This wire represents one leg, the spine and neck of our figure.

*The paper, when dry, is light and very strong of its own accord, so a strong rigid armature is inappropriate. This wire will support the figure on one leg (or arm, in the case of a figure cart-wheeling) and this gets the model off to a lively start.*

Using the fine garden wire, about 24", fold it in half and twist it around itself, so making it thicker and stronger. Make the second leg by binding this on the stiff wire at the half-way mark. If less than half-way the legs will be too short and the back too long. So, half-way then. A long single piece of thin wire will serve as shoulders and the wire arms when bound around the neck, as illustrated (**A**).

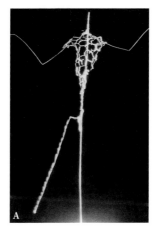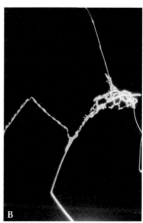

Cut a triangular piece of chicken wire about $2^{1}/2$" wide at the top and the length of a fountain pen. Curve it slightly and drop it over the neck, like a life-jacket, fold the ends over the wire shoulders and bind the lower point on to the stiff wire spine. This is our chest and rib cage.

The wire arms and legs tend to slither around annoyingly, so a generous blob of hot glue where one piece of wire touches another should fix that, plus a blob on the base. Keep your fingers where the glue cannot possibly dribble on them. Don't test it with your finger for a good five minutes. If you haven't got a glue gun (yet) then other kinds of glue should work, but they take time to dry and may not hold so well when the figure is moved about. (Sticky masking tape is better)

This is our next job, putting our figure into a lively position. By bending and curving the spine the figure becomes off balanced. This in a real figure would oblige it to do something, one leg may shoot forward, arms flung out, or back. The figure can be bent to sit or kneel. If unsure just keep bending the figure until, accidentally, it suggests something, even if it is just a person tripping over an object (a cat?) (**B**). We might get a novel idea from this hit-and-miss approach.

(6) The Dorchester Horse (detail, opposite page)

*Made for Dorchester County Museum as a school project. Four schools were involved in making the life-size horse, butcher, butcher's boy and dog to go with a period butcher's cart. The project took one month. The schools ranged from special needs to sixth form pupils and it was one of the most rewarding workshops that I have been lucky enough to participate in.*

(7) Mary Anning (Victorian Archaeologist) with dog & gulls
(8) Dog & gulls (detail)
(9) Horse, butcher & butcher's boy (full model)

## Papering

Soft, cool, damp paper, the perfect balm for the sore-fingered wiring. Mix wallpaper paste in a plastic bowl with water, (about 2 litres) until it sets to a soft jelly but stiff enough to pour out (only very slowly) when tilted, rather like Cranberry Jelly. Too stiff, add more water; too runny, more paste.

*Most cellulose wallpaper pastes are made from grass or potatoes and have a fungicide added to them which may cause problems if you have a skin condition. You would then need to wear fine plastic gloves or better, get paste from a school suppliers or from a school itself.*

## The paper

The insistent use of poor old newspaper for papier maché work is, in my opinion, why papier maché has had such a stunted contemporary history. It is used, as last resort, for theatre props and carnival floats or, worse, made into an ugly grey mush with an impossible drying requirement. Newspaper is manufactured to lie flat, to be stiff and springy; it is skillfully made to do just that, and we are asking this paper to be soft, pliable, three dimensional. No wonder there is a fight.

Kitchen roll is soft, fibrous, elastic, pliable and, best of all, doesn't disintegrate when wet. It is very affable stuff. It allows us to use our energy on the task in hand and not squander it in a struggle. I won't bang on about it any more, and I also have to tell you that I have seen some wonderful modelling done with newspaper both here and in North and South America where the battle has been most definitely won.

## Let's start

Pull a sheet off the kitchen roll. By tearing from one perforated edge to another, down the centre, we will get a clean tear. When we come to tear across the sheet it is a more ragged affair. We need these single sheets torn into quarters.

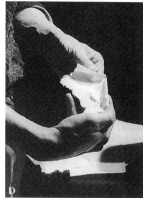

Take a scoop of paste on the tips of your fingers and smear the quarter sheet here and there, so that approximately 60% is pasted, in patches. The dry, unpasted areas will stop the paper collapsing into a slimey wadge when folded. It is rather like puff-pastry.

Fold the paper, as illustrated, about one third of the way down from the top (**C**), then fold exactly as if you were making a paper aeroplane, and pull it taught, gently through your fingers. It looks like a tiny Concorde or a Halley's Comet with it's soft, plump, pointed head and fan-like tail (**D**).

Push this point into one of the holes in the chicken wire at the shoulder of your model and, holding it there with your thumb, pull the rest across the chest and smooth down. There is a temptation to smooth, caress and press the paper, and this is exactly the right thing to do. Continue this process all over the chicken wire, with the wads of pasted paper interweaving and interlocking. To build up volume and shape, further muscle shapes are secured to this first layer, pressing and stroking as you go. Stop before the bulk becomes too flabby and dry the whole model over a current of warm air, i.e. a radiator, Aga, electric fan.

These soft, fleshy wads are the building blocks of our model. It would be easier to just bind the paper round the wire – but there are three good reasons why making this extra effort pays such dividends:

1. Folding these squashy wads secures the paper to the wire at one go.

2. By pulling the paper taut across the surface of the chicken wire we get a clean, smooth plane across the top of the wire, rather than going up and down the bumps. We leave the rough, lumpy wire and go to smooth paper surfaces in one movement.

3. Finally, this little fleshy wad is just like a tiny muscle. Were one of our own muscles to be stripped out of our bodies it would be very, very like our tiny paper one. The muscles in our long, erect bodies run, for the most part, vertically. So if we add muscle to our model following this idea then it means that however poor our knowledge of anatomy may be, we are going to end up with a figure that is 'muscular', and that must be good. The whole approach is very organic. We are modelling with tissue and cell (paper and cellulose).

I don't think it matters how roughly these wads are shaped, as long as we know what they represent. Our fingers make them by themselves after the first half dozen anyway. Too much paste and our paper turns to a slime-ball, too little and the wad begins to unfold.

Several large muscle shapes are needed for the thighs. To help the muscles stay on the wire arms and legs, a ribbon-like piece is pulled off a sheet of kitchen roll (tearing from one perforated end to the other) and run through our pasted sticky fingers. Then spin this like winding a hank of hair and it becomes a damp bootlace. Wind this long bootlace round and round the arms and legs like a pipe cleaner. It has no modelling value, but when dry it gives our muscles something to grip.

To build up the head, bind more of this bootlace around the head wire until you have a little birds egg. Keep neck, ankles and wrists thin. Sometimes it is apparent that a muscle shape isn't what we need. A hollow may need filling, or the stomach flattening, in this case one or several softly folded, pre-shaped wads are gently pressed into place. If this looks like falling off, then secure with a small piece of pasted kitchen roll bound across it, like an elastoplast. Two of these soft, plump round wads pushed together could form the buttocks (I did say this method was very organic!) Soon, a lively, muscular, figure appears before us. If very wet, dry superficially with a heat gun (or hair drier).

## Hands

Modelling hands on such a small figure is difficult. If we try making it finger by finger we could end up with a baseball glove. One method is to take a ribbon piece of kitchen roll, paste, and fold three or four times into the shape and size of a cigarette paper. Fold in the edges of one end until it describes the shape of our flat hand but minus the thumb.

Roll a long, thumb-shaped piece and bind it to the 'four finger' hand. Keeping the thumb joint well below the others (refer to your own). Squeeze the whole thing at the wrist and bind to the lower arm. Pull it into a good 'gesture' and blow dry. When bone dry and stiff we can cut two or three finger slits into this mitten, and press out the fingers or force them around, if they are to hold onto something. It is the gesture that is important, more than the modelling. If you prefer making the hand finger by finger then three fingers and a thumb look just as convincing as four. Slightly oversized hands seem to suit these little models anyway.

If you feel that you have gone as far as you can for the moment (i.e. bits are dropping off), dry it for several hours over a very warm current of air or, better, overnight on a radiator.

## Later

Now it is a different story. Strong, taut, tough and sinewy, you can improve its posture or change it completely. Standing figures can be made to sit and vice versa. No longer tentative you can pull it around as much as you need. Any damage is easily mended. You don't have to accept anything that you are not perfectly happy with. Bash back any bits of wire that have the audacity to intrude on the surface. Force it to do what you want. Don't take any nonsense. Re-smear the figure with paste where you are going to continue the modelling. Keep working at it until you have a mannequin, bald, but well modelled particularly in places that won't be covered by clothing (**E**). Even where clothes do cover, if the modelling is inadequate then the way the clothes hang may reveal it as being so. Except for a few under surfaces we can't get away with very much, I'm afraid.

**(10-12) Mermaids**

*Before and after colouring. Car sprays in cans, especially the wide range of silvers lend a very authoritative finish to some models. This figure is decorated with real seaweed which, although brittle when dried is still quite strong and very graphic and decorative.*

**(13) Tiger** (detail, opposite page)

10

11

12

Fold in a hem now as it cannot be done at any other time. Slightly pre-shape the folds with your fingers. Hold the top of the trouser leg against the model's waist and pull the trouser quite tautly down the leg (and around the knee, if the leg is bent). If fortune has smiled the folds and creases will have fallen very believably, especially if we have given them a tiny tug and a small cluster of creases have instantly appeared. These are infinitely more exquisite than anything we could hope to model ourselves. They give the impression the material is heavy and in independent movement (**F**).

We take advantage of the paper's own creases, which is why choosing the right quality of paper matters. The less we pull the paper about the better; if a piece just will not look right, discard and start again with another piece.

If you have a successful set of creases radiating from the crutch and at the knee then you are doing well. Just leave it at that and be content to patch up with small pieces of paper elsewhere. My experience has been that you can lose them by fiddling, and, once lost, they never return.

## Useful papers to have handy

*Typing paper/copy paper, poor quality thin cartridge paper, tissue paper, white paper bags (uncrumpled), thin card.*

The order in which clothes are added to the figure is the same as the figure itself would have used that morning, had it been dressed by itself i.e. shirt first, trousers then jacket. To do this we become tailors and dressmakers and emulate the way they would estimate how much material and what shape to cut it (or tear it, in our case).

## Trousers

By eye, estimate the amount and shape required for one leg and tear it out of one of the thicker papers. Damp with paste all over, both sides. It becomes limp and behaves very much like a piece of cloth. Tearing is better than cutting, as the clothes have to be made in sections and patches which need to lie across each other and join invisibly, to appear as one piece, which a feathered edge can achieve. Cutting leaves a sharp edge, impossible to disguise no matter how many times we paint it.

## Skirt or Dress

These are made in three or four pieces and can be persuaded to hang and swirl away from the body, either by being supported by fine garden wire from the underneath, or to rest on wads of soft, unpasted paper, which are later removed. It is possible too, to hold the dress in your fingers and dry it most carefully with the heat gun, until it can support itself.

Paper doilies create very pleasing lacy effects. Tear away the outside edge, it is then less easily recognised. Very lightly smear with paste and shape, but if it is too fragile and tears or collapses use several thicknesses. It also works effectively when laid on pasted typing paper. When modelled it gives the impression of heavy, embossed pattern.

## Jacket

Sleeves first, these are tubes of pasted paper. If the arms are close to the body or bent, you could fold them out straight, put on the sleeves and bend back into position when the rest of the jacket is done. The jacket is made up of three panels: left, right and back. Then collar and pocket flap. Remember to fold in the hems first.

For very thick cloth effects, like military uniforms or heavy coats or hats, double or treble the thickness of the paper, pasting each layer. Typing paper treated like this makes convincing leather boots etc. Straps and belts need a groove running along outside edges to suggest 'stitching'. This could be done with a rounded knife edge or similar. Tissue paper makes fine silk and satin effects and needs tiny taut creases pulled in.

Where a piece of material rests on the floor or against an object, tug to show how the material has been effected. Resist endlessly touching the clothes, particularly pressing them against the model. The clothes, far from making our little figure static, by showing the independent movement forced on them by the action of the body, will accent this action. Our little figure becomes livelier than ever (G).

## Emulsion

When dry, everything needs a coat of white emulsion, covering joins, filling in holes and gaps. Watered down, the paint retains detail and texture, whereas thick paint would drown it. If some clothes are painted very thickly to give them a feeling of heavy quality then a water-loaded brush licked over the top smooths away any clumsy stickiness left by thick paint.

*Again, it is these last-second 'tweaks' and tiny tugs that make so much difference. Dressing can be very quick, almost too quick; it is done before we have time to think about it. Hence this compulsion to 'fiddle', but I expect that you will have to learn the hard way, as I did.*

## Painting with Emulsion

It may seem odd to paint a white model white. When the paper dries it shrinks microscopically and although this pulls it taut and strengthens the piece, it does lose the lovely fleshy freshness it had before drying; so giving it a creamy, smooth surface with good quality emulsion goes a long way to bringing that back. Also, this emulsion, used thickly on a soft brush, fills up holes, blends one type of paper to another, lends a quality finish to clothes and can be used with water to paint areas that need the detail and texture to remain – fine wrinkles, hair and lace for example. It is possible to paint a face several times and, when dry, rub down with a fine sandpaper – giving a porcelain-like finish, useful for young and beautiful faces, hands, legs and arms.

The whole model looses its 'paperiness'. It is difficult for an observer to work out exactly what it is made of. This obliges him to see the model free of associations, and he is intrigued by so much movement, detail and changes in texture working together in one tiny object. The paint also considerably strengthens the figure. Paint sensitively, don't drown fine detail under thick paint. The model will lose its exquisiteness and there is no way to bring it back. Animals could be painted with emulsion on the fingers. This tends to make top surfaces very smooth and not get to undersurfaces, which may or may not be what you want, but is worth trying. Hair is better sprayed with a milky, watery emulsion several times if necessary, drying each time with the heat gun. It is also easier, quicker and fresher than painting.

The figure looks lovely when dry and could almost be left just there, but there is something unsatisfactory: it seems to need something else. Just what that is needs thinking about. Possible finishes are described on page 27.

**(14-17)** Three full length traffic wardens

*Concrete filled wellingtons and boots keep the figures upright and standing independently. Interesting results when placed around an expensive car in the High Street.*

14

15

16

17

18

19

## (18-19) Two cyclists

*An elderly cyclist. Take him back to when he was twenty and show him a photograph of himself as he would appear in the year 2000. Would he believe you?*

*Colourful, silvery, slithery lizards – a long way from flat caps and knickerbockers. Helmets from toys, cylinders etc., a real pleasure to make. Huge choice of bikes from the council tip.*

# Making larger heads & hands

## Head

Again, get good clear references for the head. Photographs that don't contradict each other, pinned where they can be seen alongside your modelled head. A handy stand to build the head on is a broom handle taped upright to the back of a chair, allowing us to model freely with both hands, to see it from all sides and, most importantly, work on it at eye-level.

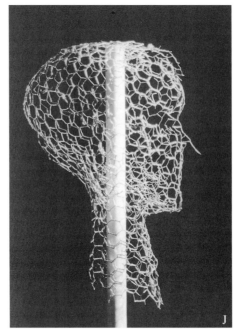

A life-sized head needs a piece of wire 12" x 9" (30cm x 23cm) and two diagonal corners pulled severely taut (**H**). This propels the wire into a curved plane. Cut this wire in five or six places (like a Union Jack). Then, wearing gloves, force it over your padded knee to make half a ball (**I**). The cut sections slide behind each other. Hold it up and see which part of the skull this could be. Back? Top? Forehead? Most likely it is the back of the head, and if this is so it will

help us to not model the back of the head too flatly, which often happens. I don't know any tricks for modelling the rest of the head, I'm afraid. There seems no other way than to bind in one wire shape to another, a strap-like piece for a jaw and chin. Another curved plane piece for the face with two horizontal slits cut close together half way down the head. These slits are pushed in above and below the cut to form sockets. A sliver of chicken wire is pulled out to support a paper nose (**J**). A nose made of chicken wire is usually too large; it certainly is when paper is added, and is almost impossible to alter. Muscles are formed from half sheets of kitchen roll and modelled trying to follow the muscle formations as they occur in a real face.

Even at this early stage we could put on lumps of paper to represent hair, and so give ourselves a taste of the finished head. Try not to get preoccupied with the face only, but work on the back and sides. Often the reason a face is not working is because we are modelling from the front only and not in three dimensions (**K**).

You also have to be prepared for the head being dead-right, first time. We have to leave it alone. Most times of course it doesn't go dead-right, but if the face has been well modelled, that is, the muscle formations have followed real muscles then you can move this head around severely, when semi-dry. Squeezed from the sides, flattened from above, supported at the jaw and pulled out again, it is amazing how it can not only survive this brutal treatment, but even look more realistic as a face.

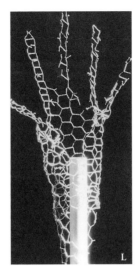
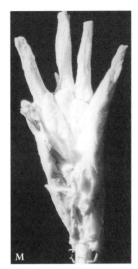
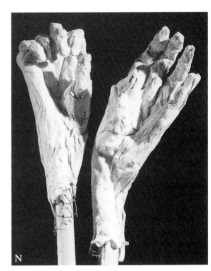

If we are making a portrait face it gives us a heaven-sent opportunity to move the face around, without necessarily losing the parts that are right, correcting big errors like head too wide or too long, forehead too prominent, chin too weak, eyes too wide apart. There are times when extreme action is the only corrective to our too tentative approach. We may also get an infinitely more interesting face than the one we had planned.

## Hands

Cut two pieces of wire about 10" x 6" (25cms x 15cms) and trim one end with tin snips. Lay your own hand on the wire and cut round it.

Make four cuts to form the fingers and thumb. Keep in mind which is to be the right hand and which the left. Wearing garden gloves, pull out the fingers, pressing in sharp spikes. The fingers then need shortening according to their position on the hand. Wrap the wrist end around the top of the broomstick (L) and, keeping the fingers star-shaped, apply long muscle shaped paper, using padded pieces for the large mound at the base of the thumb, tight, nobbly pieces for knuckles, long taught muscles running from the top of the fingers to the wrist, to account for the tendons at the back of hand (M). Dry for an hour or so then continue modelling. Stretch paper across tendons.

Typing paper added here and there will clean up surfaces and lines. Only when quite dry and finished is it a good idea to bend the fingers into position (N), patching up torn paper that has been broken as a result. Hands are particularly effective when touching the face as when the chin rests on them, or holding a cigarette.

*If we have a head and hands that we like well enough – this could give us the energy to go on to make a whole life-sized figure. If you are prepared to use real clothes this is not such a daunting task. Nevertheless, it is a lot of work and not all of it as interesting as the head and hands have been. Brace yourself for a long haul, but with the fun you can have with this figure, it will seem a small price in a retrospect.*

(20) Norman Lamont (as a Samurai puppet)
(21) Mrs Thatcher and Dennis (dancing puppet)
(22) Mrs Thatcher (detail)

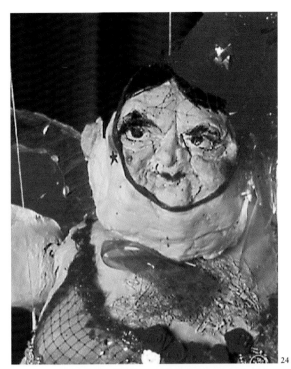

(23) Robin Cook
(24) John Prescott (detail)
(25) John Prescott

# Modelling a bird or an animal

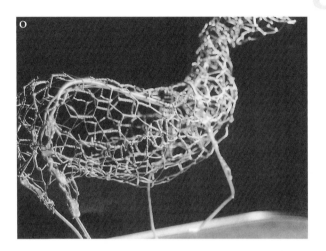

Get good photographs or drawings. Most birds and animals are similar in as much as they have an elongate, egg-shaped chest and stomach area. It is this chest, shoulders, stomach and flank shape we need first of all.

To make a model about 12" (30cms) long, we must cut a piece of chicken wire roughly 12" x 8" (30 cms x 20 cms). Take your pliers and another, similar tool because we need to push our handle through the hole at opposite and diagonal corners, and pull hard against each other. This has a pleasing effect of forcing the chicken wire into a curved plane by distorting the shape of the wire holes along this diagonal stress line. This curved plane is a wonderfully useful starting point because we now have the chest and back of an animal or the breast and stomach of a bird, or possibly its back, depending what you can see in this graphic curved plane, the back of a sitting cat perhaps.

Two such curved pieces might be juggled together to give most of the body area, plus the neck. Now we have this basic shape, we know how long the legs need to be. A horse (**O**) could stand on two legs, or even one. Birds (**P**) seem better on two. Further small pieces of chicken wire, cut into shapes and curved, if necessary, are fixed to each other with the long-nosed pliers. Where the mesh shapes lie across each other they have needle-like pieces of wire at their edges that can either be pulled from the inside and twisted over the outer, or an outer piece may be arranged in such a way that it is handily twisted around the wire beneath. These pieces need only be tacked, i.e. here and there, to be quite secure, but they do have to be done. Once the paper is on it is impossible to get at them, and the chicken wire shifts around and makes modelling with the paper a nightmare. Small features like ears, tail, hoofs, wings are best done not with the chicken wire (too crude), but with typing or kitchen roll paper. Back legs are lengths of stiff wire that will sink into deeply drilled holes in the base. Shaped as a back leg, it runs along the spine and up into the neck. There it doubles back along the same route and out of the flank, forming the second back leg.

Front legs are more wire going up into the body from a drilled hole, around the shoulders (underneath the chicken wire) and out again as the second leg. Birds are similar, with just the two legs. Everything is generously glued when in place (**Q**).

Kitchen roll again for the muscles, this time perhaps using half sheets to make longer muscles running down the neck and across the back and flank. Good reference shows the running of the muscles and as we get more involved with our animal we begin to understand why these muscles are clustered in the ways that they are. Having done this, we can stretch small pieces of kitchen roll across these muscles giving the sense of muscle under skin (**R**). (If this is the effect that we are after).

When making birds we could treat these long, narrow arrow shapes as both muscles and feathers together and apply them running from head to tail. At some point it will need to dry a little before doing more work.

## Soft Feathers

*Kitchen roll*, long muscle shapes pulled taut through the fingers until flat and sleek.

## Stiff Feathers (tail and pinion)

*Thin cartridge* or *typing paper* torn to a long, pointed shape and folded and pulled through the thumb and two first fingers forming a 'V' shape.

This 'V' running down the centre is the way grass blades are able to remain upright, and the same ingenious idea works for our long feathers (**S** – *page 26*) . Put on two or three at a time and blow dry, thus acting as as support for further feathers, exquisite engineering.

## Long curved feathers (cockerel)

Long pointed feather shapes, pasted and a long spine of thin garden wire laid as a spine. Another, similarly shaped paper laid on top and the whole semi-dried. Drive the wire up into the bird and glue. Arrange the feather and tear in several places to help the curve.

## Scales

Clumsy, roughly shaped, thickly pasted wads of kitchen roll, folded to shape, put on to overlap (as tiles on a roof) or folded and shaped and pressed on like crazy paving as in dinosaurs and crocodiles. Sand, sprinkled onto the wet emulsion and broken eggshell, gently pressed onto the surface, make excellent lizard skin texture. Split peas and small lentils sprinkled onto the loose skin around the joints, or between the plates and across the bony head are very convincing, when more white paint is added on top, as they blend all together under this thick white coat.

27

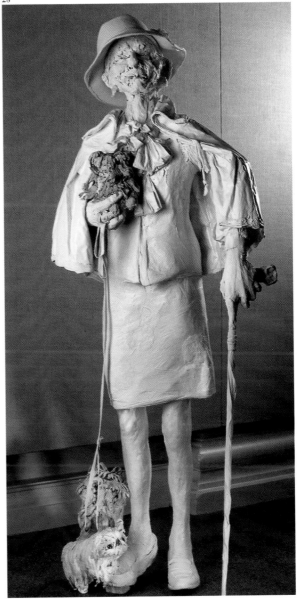

(26) Vicar and his sister (left, opposite page)

*Miss Blandford first appeared in 1985 and the vicar a year later. Initially ill-at-ease, the couple are now inseparable. Senior citizens of the 'Rush on Paper' exhibition, they have travelled Britain since 1991. They also figured in posters in junior schools where children exercised their literary skills by describing imagined lives for them.*

*Myself, I never forget they are wire and paper, but I notice that I apologise should I tread on toes etc. Like aged parents anywhere, I would like to find them a secure and permanent home.*

(27) Colonel's widow with dogs (detail)
(28) Colonel's widow with dogs

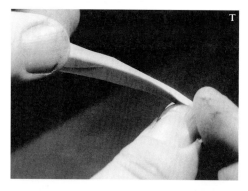
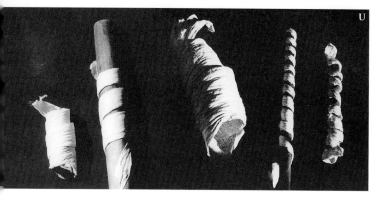

## Beaks and Claws

Typing paper folded several times to a sharp point then pulled tautly through the thumb and forefingers. Do this several times and the paper begins to curve in a most satisfying way (**T**). Another such piece gives us the lower beak, (and the bird can hold a snail or frog or fish). Claws use the same method, but are smaller, thinner and finer and also very sharply pointed.

## Hair (short)

Small pieces of kitchen roll or Kleenex dampened with paste and pulled apart leave tiny taut creases with ragged ends. Useful for hair flying away from the head or can be pasted flat (like hair gel).

## Curls and ringlets

Kitchen roll, pasted and twisted into fine string, bound round the pointed handle of a fine paint brush handle (which has itself been smeared with paste) (**U**). Slid off the handle (coiled like a spring) and pressed straight on to the pasted head of your model and allowed to uncurl down over the shoulders and back most convincingly and very feminine. A curl at a time, then gently blow dried.

## Larger curls

Brown paper or whole kitchen roll sheets bound round a pasted broom handle and slid off straight on to the model's head. Excellent for 18th Century wigs. Three kitchen roll strips can be plaited together and coiled.

## Eyes (birds, animals, reptiles)

Two black clots on a piece of stiff white paper to represent pupils, then a blob of hot glue carefully dribbled onto each – this dries almost transparently and makes convincing eyes, especially if a few specks of gold powder have been sprinkled over the dots before adding the glue. Eyebrows and lids added after the eyes are glued in place on the head.

## Fishes eyes

As above, but larger

## Cats, owls, snakes etc.

May need slits (rather than dots) as pupils.

Again – there are no rules.

Anything will do – as long as it works.

*My own approach is changing. For years I would take pleasure in finding and collecting things to add to the model. Man made or organic it didn't matter as long as it looked convincing after being painted white and blended with the rest of the sculpture. (In fact some objects, being machine made, lent a welcome authority with their clean lines, to our model).*

*Now for some reason, I am beginning to make everything out of paper (except shoes, which defeat me and I am glad to use real ones). Also, I would make my figures look as life-like as possible and now prefer them as 'tinted sculpture' (rather as black and white photographs seem more graphic than colour). It may be that in the very finished state we are presenting our model to the observer as a 'fait accompli' – now, the finish being more 'tinted' and 'suggested' his and her own imagination is brought into play completing the image.*

My own preference for the model is 92% sculpture and the rest hinted at through colour and pattern. This 8% though, is most potent. The colour and hue of a face, particularly cheeks and cheekbones give a direct insight into the emotional and physical state of the personality we are trying to portray, plus their 'taste'.

Colour, to my mind, is best 'pastel' and the use of strong colour used in a very limited and targeted way. Small models can't take much strong colour – and if coupled with clumsy painting are just horrible and disappointing. After all that work we should not then lose them because of this.

Raw black and red, straight form the tube are the worst offenders. Black mixed with white to become dark grey will read as black anyway and with a little blue or green or brown becomes a colour in its own right.

You might like to mix colour by dabbing a big blob of white emulsion into the middle of a piece of scrap, strong white paper and surrounding it with small smears of primary colours, these are introduced to the edge of the white

emulsion blob. If you don't like the way the colour is going you can start again without having wasted too much. Once you hit the colour you are after – then you know how to mix more of it.

Paint this colour thickly, or not so thickly, but not thinly, not watery. The paint runs off the top surfaces and ledges into the cracks and crevasses, highlighting them and exaggerating everything, plus looking scruffy. It gives a poor 'reading' of the model. The paint should be fresh, even and smooth. Where one colour comes up against another the edge should be clean, not ragged, it doesn't have to be perfectly even but no little flecks of white undercoat should show through. On a particularly rough or undulating surface paint first with a watery colour (or spray with a diffuser) to get into the cracks and fissures, then paint with a thicker coat, possibly two or three times, until it looks and feels right.

## Flesh colour

A tiny drop of crimson, another of light or mid-yellow on a sheet of strong white paper. Add a tiny bit of crimson to the edge of the white and mix – this makes a strawberry ice cream, then introduce yellow: juggling these two colours with the white will produce a fresh healthy flesh colour. You can cool it down with a tiny touch of green if too healthy, then test it on the model.

When painting life-size I paint the whole head and neck and hands with an even coat of light, fawn/brown, the colour of a light brown chicken egg. When dry, I have crimson (carmine) and yellow (canary) ink in two small puddles on a sheet of tough white paper and a big pot of fresh clean water. With a big soft brush introduce a tiny touch of red to the yellow ink and with plenty of water on the brush wash it on to the face. Sometimes adding more red, sometimes less. The ink stays on the face and also runs into cracks and crevasses, which might be helpful. The underlying fawn colour is apparent beneath the translucent inks and this effect is surprisingly life-like. Intensify the red for ears, nose, cheeks, neck but if you overdo it you may have to go all the way back to painting the head light fawn/brown and starting again.

30

31

(29) From Hogarth's 'Marriage a la mode' (left, opposite page)

(30) Queen Elizabeth II

(31) George IV, 'Prinny' (life-size)

*Somebody wrote in their diary at the time 'Today His Majesty did take off his stays and his stomach did touch his knees!' Wonderfully dainty on his feet and dainty in his movements for such a fat man. This is the fourth George IV I have made and still haven't got him!*

# Masks, theatre props, wigs & hats

For making the above I know of nothing better than our good friend the kitchen roll. It is fast, light, robust and easily mended when damaged.

## Animal masks

If this mask has a long snout, then it is going to need strong fencing wire as an armature. Chicken wire stretched over this and glue gummed in place. A skin of thick, soft wads of pasted kitchen roll cover the outside, modelling as you go.

When dry, the head can be turned upside down and more thick wads applied firmly to the inside. This is for comfort for the wearer and to protect him or her from nasty bits of

wire poking through. If the person who is to wear this mask is available, then the mask can be custom made. Two large eye holes need cutting out and metal tea strainers (mesh) pushed and glued into these gaps. If they are correctly positioned, the wearer has surprisingly good vision. They also help ventilate the mask, as wearers often complain that these masks, although comfortable and light, can get very hot inside, so if it is possible to have a disguised hole in the top, then please do this.

The mask can be made to fit firmly and comfortably and so free the wearer from the need for straps etc. The tea strainers can be painted realistically as eyes, the wearer's face cannot be seen through this painted mesh.

Nose, ears and teeth might be best made from foam rubber, this being able to take being endlessly knocked, whereas paper would crack and crumble. The foam can be painted along with the rest of the mask (by adding a tiny drop of washing up liquid to the paint it will cover the foam more easily). Painting the mask thickly with white emulsion will strengthen it, but because the kitchen roll can give such sensitive fur and leather effects, you may prefer to just spray it as it is. Being easily damaged like this you might keep it in its own box. A long slice of hot water bottle and you have a lolling tongue.

## Theatre Props

Kitchen roll smeared with paste, pulled and folded diagonally, pulled through the fingers until flat and added to a fencing wire armature will make scrolls and twists, fishtail florettes, representing wrought iron work (**V**). Painted with black matt emulsion, sprayed or painted silver and painted again with watery matt black emulsion. Rub lightly, when dry, to expose the silver underneath slightly. The same approach would be used for gold and brass work on furniture, picture frames, sword and door handles, candle sticks, hinges etc. but with a finer use of paper. Sprayed with gold and toned down with a watery sepia, (rather than black).

## Jewellery

The glue gun comes in to its own when making jewellery, fine filigree silver and gold lace or embossing, embroidering or piping on clothes and uniforms (**W**). The method is to dribble hot glue from the gun from a height of several feet into a plate or saucer that has about an inch of water in it.

For costume jewellery, take a coloured marble and wrap it in a cloth. Give it a clout with a hammer on the ground and from the shattered marble, choose any pieces that look like jewels. Make a mount from garden wire, if it is to be worn as a ring or tiara or bracelet, and surround with glue from the gun to look like a mount. When this glue is painted silver or gold – you will have something that could easily be mistaken for the Crown Jewels. An iridescent marble is particularly effective.

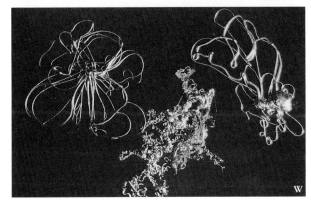

With the glue gun, you can also draw directly on to material, or on to the collar and cuffs of a jacket, and run piping around the edges. A little gold powder puffed on to this whilst still hot is effective, (and so quick!).

## Wigs - Judges, 17th and 18th Century court figures (Dread locks etc.)

Chicken wire, shaped to the head (pieces firmly joined together), papered with soft, well pasted kitchen roll wads inside and out. Elaborate wigs need a further chicken wire shaped armature, well secured to the head shape.

The method is the same as for making ringlets i.e. a piece of kitchen roll, smeared with paste, folded diagonally and pulled flat through the fingers. This is bound round the end of a broomstick handle that is already smeared with paste.

Slide the ringlets off by pushing straight on to its place on the head. Try not to crush or handle unnecessarily. Dry partially with heat gun after every two or three curls and glue gun them where the glue cannot be seen. Be generous with these curls, have lots, and also have a good reference. Make a hinge of string or tape, if ringlets have to hang freely down the back or across the shoulders. Spray a watery white or creamy white several times: puff on a little mother of pearl glitter, whilst the paint is still wet, and your wig will be powdered.

## Hats for theatre or for models

A chicken wire frame is usually too clumsy, but if you are going to make a huge hat, there isn't much alternative. Card is a bit floppy unless it is secured, as in a tricorn hat. The usual kitchen roll wads inside and out, squeezed as flat as possible, and flat pasted sheets laid on top to look like felt or leather when dry. Kitchen roll pulled into string can be coiled around to look like straw. You can make:

*Flowers from soft or stiff paper.*
*Ribbon from cartridge paper.*
*Bows from typing paper* (smeared both sides, the edges folded in as a hem, and treated as though real material) (**X**).

The good thing is, that the hats always fit perfectly, if they have been actually made on the model's head.

Paper table cloths make very good clothing when pasted. Good scarves, stoles, cloaks etc for paper models.

Models are usually better in paper shirts than real ones. Paper is pasted double and folded, then pressed around the neck. If it fits comfortably and with the tips of the collar slightly curled, it looks as though the model has worn it for some time.

(32) Nelson Mandela

(33) Pope John Paul II

(34) Ron and Nancy Reagan (right, opposite page)

*These puppets come to pieces and will pack into a
surprisingly small basket, using plastic overflow
pipe and the variety of connecting joints. They hang
from a spring and will square dance back and forth.
As Ron and Nancy had five face-lifts between them,
they are easily captured in paper.*

33

32

If I was going to have any hope at all in persuading you to embark on making a life size figure, I would have to give you some good reasons for doing so, because it is quite a long haul. It has to be done as well as one is able – or you will never be free of it – and it has to be finished.

One of the rewards comes in the form of learning a lot about the human figure, about personalities (and how this echoes in their skin textures) and about aging. It comes in the form of insights and confirms for us things already half-known.

To midwife a complete figure successfully brings with it a quiet joy of achievement. There is a lot of fun to be had with the figure afterwards; even a clumsily made figure has the ability to momentarily appear real to people coming across it in an unguarded moment. Perhaps, most important of all, it shows us with inescapable clarity the stance we take towards other people and, by the same stroke, ourselves, and this information has to be worth having, however sobering.

## Starting...

I have got into the habit of making head and hands first to encourage me to go on to finish, if I like them enough. Unfortunately, I can't get out of this approach, although I am sure the figure should be tackled comprehensively. I suggest you set about making the whole figure at one go, as this is the correct way.

Two long lengths of ½" plastic overflow pipe, plus connecting points make a marvellous skeleton. It is curiously cheap too! Easy to cut with a hacksaw it can be pieced together with joints (T shape, 45° or 90°). You may prefer to keep the arms and leg joints loosely joined. This means it can sit anywhere (and can travel in a car as a passenger).

If it is to stand, the legs are better kept as straight lengths of pipe. To make a figure free-standing you need an old pair of neat Wellingtons (not huge, clumsy things) and fill them half full of concrete and small rubble, setting a 3 foot length of pipe into each. If they feel unstable, you may need to cut little wedges of wood and stick under the base of the boot.

Even though your figure may stand up O.K. it won't be stable if knocked or if a gust of wind takes it. So perhaps you can devise a third resting point like a walking stick or even a little dog (if you could get a metal rod running through from one of the dog's feet, out through his neck at the collar, then continue as the 'lead' up into the model's hand, up through his arm 'pipes', across his shoulder and through a hole in his spine 'pipe'.

A figure that is loose-jointed needs a real jacket and trousers (or skirt) and to get the jacket on and off, one arm has to be able to detach at the shoulder. The plastic joints are excellent for this, since we just push them on and pull them off. Where the joints are to move, we must make our own wire connections. Myself, having low engineering skills, I make joints with wire by drilling through the pipe. Plastic garden chain from garden centres also works well.

A figure, that is to be fat, may need a more supportive spine. Plastic piping is easily cut or easily extended, with the right connecting piece, so none of these measurements are unalterable.

Two pieces of chicken wire approx 1 metre x 60cms are required. The shorter edge is pinned by your heel onto the floor and the other end pulled hard with both hands. This gives us our working curved plane, which creates our chest and back. Juggle them around and attach them together, thinner at the waist, around the spine. They need wiring to the shoulders and spine, and hot glue dribbled here and there until stable.

Thighs are the same, but smaller and need buttocks which can be shaped around the knee (page 18). Binding these various pieces of chicken wire together takes the time, especially bending in all the nasty little bits of wire that will otherwise catch at you. The lower arms and legs are more easily modelled and now the head and hands can be modelled (pages 18 & 19).

If you use real shoes then scrap chicken wire can be rammed in and glue dribbled, attaching the shoe to the leg pipe by drilling a hole through the pipe, and a wire going through this and down into the shoe, and possibly even going through the shoe itself.

All this work takes time and is very fiddly. I do it outside in the sun or listen to the radio.

## Papering

You need plenty of kitchen roll, a small table on which you can put a flat board, or better, a slab of plate glass, and a bucket of paste. It is quicker and easier if you tear the kitchen roll at every three sheets, placing them on top of each other, then tearing these thick wads into three. Easier than tearing one at a time with sticky hands.

The torso and legs need a skin of kitchen roll over the whole area. When this is dry, we can set about putting on the paper in the form of muscles. This is exactly the same as the smaller figure, except that the 'muscles' are necessarily larger and longer. If we use the illustration as a very rough guide, we are bound to get a believable muscled figure.

Muscles are made as illustrated (page 10). Notice that Nature is not symmetrical. The lower legs for instance, their widest points are not opposite each other, like a jug but slightly diagonal. Nearly all the muscles run up and down the body, except for muscles running across the barrel of the chest.

Just be brave, follow muscle patterns as best you can. Where they are in danger of falling off, bind them on with more paper around them: you may put 'skin' over some parts; this has the very pleasing effect of 'skin over muscle', because that is exactly what it is.

Sometimes you need to work in great wads of pasted paper, when building up bulk or filling in dips. Dry often with a blow heater of some kind. Your fingers will tell you when things are beginning to feel right. Just keep going, until you are sure you have dealt with its worst aspects – because if you have a figure sitting there in its thermal underwear and it looks O.K., then how much better is it going to be when dressed?

## Faces

Some notes from my own observations of where various personal characteristics might display themselves in the face. I would say that *discrimination* tends to show itself at the eyebrow and the muscles that operate it and *intelligence and compassion* is in the shadow in the eye thrown by the eyelid. *Humour* (seeing two or more aspects of a situation simultaneously) may be at the corner of the eye. The nose indicates the kind of interest a person takes in his world.

The muscles that lead to the base of the nose show quite clearly a person's attitude to himself, especially marked in self-satisfied and fastidious people. (It has something to do with the passage of air to the nose). *Vanity* seems to hover around the hair falling across the forehead, if it does. *Seediness* is there at the hair behind the ear and *disappointment* at the jowls. Lips show the kind of *generosity*, or lack of it. The back of the neck will focus a person not in touch with him or herself and perhaps the opposite is true also. *Sexuality* fizzes across the cheekbone, jawbone and outer muscles of the neck, (and many other places as well).

(35-38) Salisbury Cathedral nativity figures

*Four of six angels made to fly above the Crib in Salisbury Cathedral. This Nativity scene has grown each year with the addition of more figures over eight years.*

36

37

38

Those committed to service to their fellow men have a lovely, silvery light colour of skin, eyes and hair. The same quality expressing itself through an *impulsive* person is more likely to be warm, rich, dark and lustrous. *Tenacity* might be there at the chin, and people, unlucky enough to be in constant physical pain, seem to have the colour drained out of them, and *psychological pain* turns the skin pappy.

It is interesting that qualities like **intelligence, innocence, compassion** and **courage** cannot be caricatured. The joke backfires on its perpetrator, whereas **self-satisfaction, pomposity, lewdness, servility, humourlessness, indolence** and the like cannot be too savagely attacked.

## General Notes on Dressing

I have suggested making **collars, cuffs of shirts** and **blouses** from paper as they fit so comfortably and blend so well. You may also need to make **shirt fronts** and **waistcoats** from paper where they show under a real jacket. Paper doilies make excellent **lace**, and pressed onto a sheet of pasted cartridge paper can make useful embossed, patterned material.

It seems that paper people are as fussy as flesh ones when it comes to choosing clothes that will suit them, and you may have to do much trawling of jumble sales etc. **The Queen Mother** model, for instance, sent me everywhere looking for dress material – I went up to London especially – but failed to find it. In the end I bought some plain, silky, cream nylon material and painted on huge turquoise roses. There are times when even real things don't look real. If you use a real watch, for example, on a model, you have to go to all the trouble of painting it white on the models wrist, then paint it to look like a watch.

*Jewellery* made with a glue gun is impressive. By using broken glass marbles you can afford to be very generous with your diamonds, rubies and emeralds in their heavy gold settings. *Real spectacles* rarely look right, unless the frames are very fine, but sometimes thick lenses will magnify the eyes most effectively. It may be, that taking the lenses out of their heavy frames and setting them in frames of your own, made from thin garden wire and the glue gun, will be enough.

*Figures on bicycles* are good fun. You may need to spoof the bicycles up a bit. You can buy a perfectly good bicycle from your local Council tip for the price of a pound of apples, such is our breathtaking wastefulness.

A trip to the dump nudges the imagination by coming across old luggage, or exercise bikes or dentist chairs, vacuum cleaners, cocktail cabinets and so on, all possible starting points.

As with telling a story you can spoil it with too much detail. The point gets lost somewhere along the line. In the same way our model needs editing, that is, keep the point of the model in your mind, and only use things that help discard the irrelevant, however interesting. Don't overkill. Leave something for the observer to find.

Store the models in big plastic bags. Dust will take all the freshness from them and mice can eat a whole hand or half a face. The models need periodic freshening up, which is easy and is a pleasure to do.

# Notes for teachers

I have said elsewhere in this book that children take to this kind of modelling like ducks to water. It moves at their own speed (fast) and needs no special technicalities that might hang up this forward momentum. The intervals needed for drying the figures also seems to happily parallel the times when they need to break for themselves. Children never lose sight of their figure, right from the moment the wire skeleton is up in action. Going from one stage to another the 'new' soon makes itself apparent and so draws them on. Children that work slowly or more hesitantly can easily see from the work of their friends what the next stage is and this, by itself, gives confidence.

*If you are to take a whole class yourself, if you can get any kind of help whatsoever, it will be of great benefit. Someone, any adult or older child who, just by being older, is more dextrous, not necessarily artistic, just to help wobbly models regain their shape and posture.*

During the last twenty years or so I must have run some hundreds of workshops, mostly in schools where there can sometimes be a hundred children or more, usually in a big hall, and the help that volunteer Mums can give, cannot be underestimated. They have saved my bacon so many times and I take my hat off to them here. Recognising a need and seeing the children occupied and so involved, they have come up with just the right help. Even some teachers, who have viewed the whole workshop slightly askance on seeing power drills, scratchy wire, pliers, glue guns, hot air driers, and emulsion paint, have come round at the sight of such lively application and concentration. It has to do with the medium being so simple and organic, each child making his own observations (some very revealing) and the timing of it all

seems just about right. Two whole days (plus a possible extra morning at a later date to finish detail and background). Although, done two lessons at a time also seems to work, the models drying naturally between lessons.

This next section describes a school workshop from beginning to end. Something that used to play heavily on my mind was:

If there is a hall full of children all in their old clothes, normal lessons suspended for two days, and they decide to make a holiday of it and fool about, what then could I, a stranger to them, do? Nothing, is the answer.

What happens initially, I notice, is that the noise does tend to crescendo and then drops back, as the requirements and disciplines of making the figure take over. Then there is a great moment when a bubbling, lively murmur is the sound coming off the hall, like bacon sizzling gently in the pan. I know then it is OK, it is looking after itself, I am not

**(39-42) Three figures on a trike**

*At first the solitary gentleman peddalled laboriously in a slow circle, the trike being driven by the engine of a truck windscreen wiper and car battery in a basket behind him. Also on board a tray of seed potatoes and a fork wrapped in a sack. He was off to the allotment when his wife insisted on coming along. They picked up a friend and all this proved too much for the game little engine. They haven't moved since.*

**(43) New-age travellers** (detail, opposite page)

*Her hair is made from brass, steel and aluminium swarf from a scrap yard.*

39

40

41

42

required to concern myself at all. If there is a monkey (or two), I have learnt not to interfere because firstly, he or she soon finds that they are not getting the usual response, the others being more interested in what they are doing and secondly, their own model is beginning to look pretty sick; their egos don't like that at all and so begin to get stuck in. Also, you will be surprised that models that don't seem to be going anywhere, can be quite transformed in the last half hour, and you didn't even see it happen.

A 'theme' is a useful starting point, especially if previously researched, usually connected to the National Curriculum.

## Birds

Very good for younger children. Perhaps a life-size old man, made by older children, having his lunch on a bench and covered in small birds made by the younger ones.

*Cockerels, Ducks, Parrots, Peacocks.*
Birds could be displayed in a branch of a tree.

## Animals

*Jungle, Domestic, St. Francis, Noah, Dinosaurs.*

## People

*People and their tools of work.*
*Knights & Ladies, battle scenes, castle.*
*Nativity – many camels, sheep, donkeys, Arabs, Kings etc...*
*Emphasis on balance/unbalanced.*
*Action/reaction – one thing affecting another.*

Try to work all together in one room, you won't have to repeat and children can overhear you talking to someone else, and they learn a lot from each other.

## You need...

*Wooden blocks* about 15cms x 8cms x 2cms deep, mixed with larger and different shapes.
*Electric* and *hand drill* with several bits.
*Fencing wire* – from garden Centres, Farm Suppliers.
*Thin green plastic coated wire* used for tying plants.
*Chicken wire*, fine gauge.
*Wallpaper paste from Consortium.* Otherwise commercial cellulose paste, but this does have a fungicide in it, which may affect a child with a skin allergy.
*Glue gun* or *cool gun.*
*Long nosed pliers, ordinary pliers.*
*Tin snips* or *all purpose cutters* or *big old scissors* (for chicken wire).
*Leather garden gloves.*

The instructions are as those earlier in the book (pages 6-15).

*Children can cut their own fencing wire if they squeeze the pliers with both hands and can manage to make a small bite into this wire. By placing the head of the pliers perfectly flush with this notch and wiggling the short wire up and down, the wire must break here. The pliers must be exactly flush. Young children need help, and it does take time but it gives them great satisfaction to be able to do this. Make the wire skeleton and add the chicken wire rib cage (page 7). If you haven't a glue gun, small pieces of masking tape around the joints is the next best thing. All this takes about 1½ hours.*

Demonstrate making a skeleton of your own for them to watch. They can then refer to it without having to trouble you. You will need to show them the papering technique on it too.

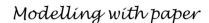

## Modelling with paper

*Goodish quality white kitchen roll*
(not patterned of coloured).

*Typing paper, copy, white paper bags, poor quality, thin cartridge paper.*

Very young children may have trouble with these aeroplane shapes but could manage paper folded more simply, as suggested here. If left to apply paper without using any kind of shaping, the obvious way to do it would be to bind and wrap paper round and round the skeleton. This has no modelling value and it is soon apparent. Perhaps this is a good moment to ask them to feel their muscles, take up the posture of their figure themselves, and they can feel which of their muscles are taut, and which relaxed.

In school workshops we are usually getting ready for lunch now and all the wet paper models are collected together in a huddle and covered with sheets of newspaper like an igloo. This, with a blow heater at one end is a perfect drying tent, the moisture passing through the newspaper but most of the heat remaining inside.

Carry on as suggested on page 18 with hands, hair and make a start on the clothing (page 14). At the end of the day the models are wet, vulnerable and in serious need of overnight drying over radiators, Agas, blow heaters, etc., any current of warm air.

The next morning it is a different story. Tough, strong, no question of paper dropping off, the children can alter and pull their models about with impunity, if they need to.

Postures altered, limbs shortened or lengthened. Figures need to be smeared with paste for the new paper to stick to the old.

When finished and dressed, the figures need drying individually for ten minutes or so with hair dryer or similar, preparing them for painting with white emulsion. The most effective (and fun) way of painting is to set up a table outside, if possible, covered with plastic sheet and newspaper, a dish, or several with an inch or two of emulsion in each. Then the children can be encouraged to paint the model with their fingers, rubbing it in like sun lotion, avoiding things like dresses if they are made with doilies. As one child finishes, so fresh newspaper is just pressed onto the paint splashed work area. Children really need to be in very old clothes. Aprons can help spread paint and are better not used, they also have to be washed after. My experience is that some children just love the thick creamy paint and do get in a mess, but nothing that can't be washed off, if dealt with whilst still wet. Several buckets of warm water near the table enable them to clean themselves up before going back into school. Any patterned kitchen rolls can be used up here.

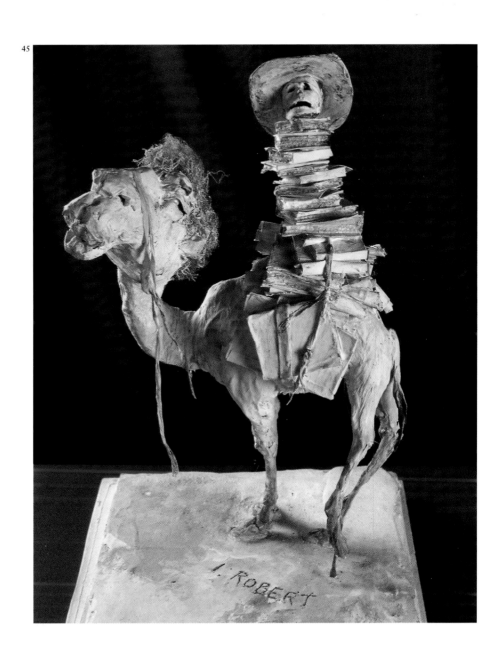

(44) John Middleton Murray, Katherine Mansfield,
D.H. Lawrence and Frieda (left, opposite page)

(45) Robert Graves

Also a small fine brush gives them a chance to paint inside crevasses, and avoid little give-away flecks of white showing through. It is a help if you show them how to make skin colour. A blob of white on a scrap of paper with a tiny squirt of yellow on one side and red on the other. Mix in a little red into the edge of the white and you will get strawberry ice cream, then introduce a tiny touch of yellow to this, and a nice healthy skin colour begins to appear.

If not, then it is a matter of juggling these three paints until something suitable appears. You need very little. Encourage clean edging where one colour comes up against another and keep any patternwork just lightly suggested, rather than mechanically repeated.

## Spraying

Using the spray diffuser is another way around the painting problem. Cups of watery paint or ink in four or five different colours are prepared ready and a spraying area set aside, with plastic sheeting around and behind a box to stand the model on at face height. It takes a fierce blow to get the diffuser to spray the paint, but it only takes a second or two to cover one side of the model, before it needs turning and the other side sprayed. they can just about do it. If not, it may be that the paint is too thick to go through the diffuser, or it has become blocked with sediment.

A figure can be masked by wrapping a piece of kitchen roll around the top and the figure painted in two or three colours, without any need to clean the diffuser. This spraying is surprisingly delicate and very pretty. The ideal way to treat dainty dresses. I have a little electric compressor and insert the diffuser's mouth piece down the pipe, thus avoiding this apoplectic blowing. If you show them beforehand how the diffuser works, they tend to be fascinated especially if you tell them it is amongst the oldest tools known to man, along with the scraper and the stone axe. Our forefathers, living in caves, mixed a little sooty water in a clay vessel and with a

Emulsion has a self-drying facility, which is useful, but the models need to be dried again properly with blow heaters. Several can be clustered together and dried by one person with a a hair drier for ten minutes or so. They look lovely. Fresh and white. There is a good argument for just leaving them like this, but, if they thought you were going to short-circuit the final painting, you would be in trouble. Another reason for wishing they could be left just white is that they are exquisite like this, but children, unskilled at painting, especially three dimensional surfaces and using thick paint straight from the tube with big old bristly brushes, just obliterate the model, particularly exacerbated though the use of pure black. With this in mind, to minimise damage and disappointment, I give them a sheet of typing or old computer paper to use as a pallet and plop a big dollop of emulsion in the middle with a table spoon. Then place around it a mean little squirt of four or five colours, avoiding black. To get any bulk at all the children are obliged to mix the colour with emulsion, thus getting only a pastel colour, which is a much better base colour for a small model, where pink will read as red, dark grey (green, red and blue) will read as black, etc.

bent piece of dried grass did exactly what we are doing with our diffusers. They put their outstretched hands against the cave wall and blew, leaving a negative impression of their hands. (Many of these imprints show fingers missing at joints and nobody seems to have an explanation for this). All this brings us to the end of the second day. Those who finish quickly, go on to work on the 'environment', that is, the base, so there is a little theatrical scene there: a vignette. If birds have been made then *nests* from twigs and dried grass. *Eggs* from plasticine, *worms, snails, frogs* hanging from *beaks.*

For human figures it is usually *goal posts, grass, roads, paths, gates, dustbins, bottles (for drunks), skate boards* and so on.

## Useful materials

*Paper doilies, straws* that bend at right angles to goal posts, machine guns, drain pipes. *Nets* from oranges, *Split peas, lentils, broken egg shells* for dinosaur skin, sprinkled on to the wet emulsion. *Silvered hologram paper* for armour, evergreen foliage, good for trees and bushes. *Glitter* for dancers' dresses, spice girls, ice rinks. *Gold paint. Ping pong balls* for footballs and cut open for helmets.

When all the mess is cleared away, and they are displayed quietly on dark paper you begin to appreciate a lot of the detail you may have missed in all the activity earlier. Parents also get a new look at their offspring, when they see what has been made.

# Acknowledgements & credits

This book is dedicated to my parents Geraldine and Philip Rush for their unswerving kindness to myself and others.

## Acknowledgements

I would like to acknowledge some of the generous help I have had over the years in connection with this work:

**Fanny, Joe** and **Sam,** who grew up with my preoccupation with all this

**Jane Deacon** for her early support

**Mark Eynon** who introduced the work to the Henley Festival

**Caroline Mornement** for keeping the whole thing up and running

**John Sanson** for cheerful support

**Liz Sanson** for the open-handed gift of studio space to work in

**Belinda**

Thoughful proof reading by **Lyndon Jones**

**Jon Atkinson,** fellow toiler

**Christine Kapteijn** and **The Surrey Institute of Art & Design, University College,** who have made it possible for this book to happen

## Credits

Photography
**Harry Richards** – no. 37 and 38

**Simon Sandys** – no. 1-9, 13-25, 27-32, 35-36, 43-45
By courtesy of Leicester City Museum & Art Gallery

**Harry Richards** and **Sue Tarrant** of **Bryanston School, ATV Deptartment** – black and white pictures

**Fanny Rush** – back page

Design
**Nimbus Design and Communications**
(www.nimbusdesign.co.uk)

Printing
**Craft Print Pte Ltd., Singapore**